A Moment with God

For:
Jacob McAllister

From:
E Bruce Harvey, Jr.
Brittany Harvey
2014

Other books in this series:

A Moment with God FOR TEENS

A Moment with God FOR THOSE WHO GRIEVE

A Moment with God FOR SUNDAY SCHOOL TEACHERS

A Moment with God FOR TEACHERS

A Moment with God FOR MOTHERS

A Moment with God for Graduates

PRAYERS FOR EVERY GRADUATE

Maribeth Walker

Abingdon Press
Nashville

A Moment with God for Graduates

PRAYERS FOR EVERY GRADUATE

Copyright © 2011 by Abingdon Press

All rights reserved.
No part of this work may be reproduced or transmitted in any form or by any means, electronic or mechanical, including photocopying and recording, or by any information storage or retrieval system, except as may be expressly permitted by the 1976 Copyright Act or in writing from the publisher. Requests for permission should be addressed to Permissions, The United Methodist Publishing House, P.O. Box 801, 201 Eighth Avenue South, Nashville, TN 37202-0801 or permissions@umpublishing.org.

This book is printed on acid-free paper.

ISBN 978-1-4267-4588-1

Scripture quotations are from the Common English Bible. Copyright © 2011 by the Common English Bible. All rights reserved. Used by permission. (www.CommonEnglishBible.com)

11 12 13 14 15 16 17 18 19 20—10 9 8 7 6 5 4 3 2 1

MANUFACTURED IN MEXICO

CONTENTS

Knowing You	8
Certainty	10
Making Plans	12
Make Me Rich	14
No Harm, No Foul	16
Hope	18
Facing the Future	20
No Strings Attached	22
Pressing On	24
Strange Days	26
Gratitude	28
I Need Wisdom	30
Making a Difference	32
I'm Hurting	34
Making Decisions	36
Nursing a Grudge	38
Going to Church	40
Ready for Prayer	42

Contents

Temptation	44
In the Know	46
Finding Purpose	48
New Friends	50
Expressing My Anger	52
Social Action	54
Foot in Mouth	56
Sing a Song of Praise	58
Walking in the Spirit	60
Trust	62
Trouble	64
No Fear	66
New Ideas	68
Loneliness	70
Distractions	72
Hand-Me-Downs	74
Undercover Christian	76
A Real Job	78
Best Book	80
First Impressions	82

Contents

Armor of God	84
Earning Extra Credit	86
Inconvenience	88
Changing the World	90
Meeting the Requirements	92
Blank Slate	94
Gentleness	96
High Anxiety	98
Praiseworthy Things	100
Silent Prayer	102
Doubts	104
Living Praise	106
A New Day	108
Surprise Ending	110
Amazing Grace	112
The Gift of Laughter	114
Accountability	116
Priorities	118
A Childlike Faith	120
Obedience	122

Knowing You

"I know the plans *I* have in mind for you, declares the LORD; they are plans for peace, not disaster, to give you a future filled with hope."

—JEREMIAH 29:11 (emphasis added)

YOU KNOW, LORD. I think I know myself—my heart, my plans—but I'm only guessing, and sometimes I surprise myself. You know all about me and love me more than I can imagine. You knew yesterday who I would be today, and you know today who I'll be tomorrow. And yet, you could never love me any more or any less than you do in this moment.

Maybe I don't need to know myself as well as I thought. Maybe I really need to focus on knowing you; who knows, I may even discover myself in the process. Teach me to know you, God, and show me what it is you see in me.

Certainty

"I *know* the plans I have in mind for you, declares the LORD; they are plans for peace, not disaster, to give you a future filled with hope."

—JEREMIAH 29:11 (emphasis added)

WHEN I THINK about the future, I think about wishes, hopes, dreams, plans. And I have to admit, Lord, I also think about questions, worries, and fears. I only wonder about what will happen next; but you know. I find a lot of comfort in that, God. I know I'm not just wishing on a star or keeping my fingers crossed, because you know. I pray that I'll keep trusting in what you know.

I only wonder about what will happen next; but you know. I find a lot of comfort in that, God. I know I'm not just wishing on a star or keeping my fingers crossed, because you know.

Making Plans

"I know the *plans* I have in mind for you, declares the LORD; they are plans for peace, not disaster, to give you a future filled with hope."

—JEREMIAH 29:11 (emphasis added)

DEAR GOD, everyone I talk to asks about my future plans—family, friends, even people I barely know. Sometimes I'm not sure what to say; the few plans I've made seem practical one day and ridiculous the next. How wonderful to realize that you have plans for my life!

Someone told me that planning should really be prayer with a pencil in your hand. That's what I want, Lord. I want to find and follow your plan. Help me seek it every step of the way.

Make Me Rich

"I know the *plans* I have in mind for you,
declares the LORD; they are plans for peace,
not disaster, to give you a
future filled with hope."

—JEREMIAH 29:11 (emphasis added)

I KNOW MONEY doesn't buy happiness, God, but still, I wouldn't mind being rich and having all the things money can buy. This seems to be what a lot of people expect from me now: I'm a graduate; I'm supposed to work toward having lots of money and things.

But your promise is even better than that, Lord. You promise to prosper me. That means not necessarily being rich in money, but something even better: having a rich life. Keeping my eyes on you and on your spiritual riches will take a lot of focus. But I know I can do it if you'll help me.

No Harm, No Foul

"I know the plans I have in mind for you, declares the LORD; they are plans for peace, *not disaster*, to give you a future filled with hope."

—JEREMIAH 29:11 (emphasis added)

MERCIFUL GOD, I can't understand your forgiveness. I haven't always followed you as faithfully as I should. I have even tried, from time to time, to reject you and what I've been taught. I have a real stubborn streak, and I want to go my own way.

But thanks to Jesus Christ, none of that matters to you. He makes me acceptable to you. You don't want to seek revenge. You don't want to throw rocks on me when I feel like I'm down in a hole. You just want to love me. I really appreciate that.

Hope

"I know the plans I have in mind for you,
declares the LORD; they are plans for peace,
not disaster, to give you a
future filled with *hope*."

—JEREMIAH 29:11 (emphasis added)

SOMEHOW I've come this far, God. But—what if? What if things don't work out like I planned? What if I fail? What if all of this was for nothing? What if something happens that I could never have dreamed of in a million years? What if I don't know what to do? What if. . . ?

You give me hope. What a wonderful word, and what a wonderful gift. Some days I just can't manufacture hope myself, God. But you give hope to me; like a beautifully wrapped present with a big bow on top, it's mine for the unwrapping. And that's what makes me able to carry on: you, me, and hope.

Facing the Future

"I know the plans I have in mind for you,
declares the LORD; they are plans for peace,
not disaster, to give you a
future filled with hope."

—JEREMIAH 29:11 (emphasis added)

SOMETIMES *FUTURE* is a scary word, to me, Lord; too many uncertainties. Uncharted paths, unfamiliar waters, the great unknown; all these cliches seem to apply when I think about the future. It seems like this vast expanse of years stretching out before me, and I have no idea at all about how to approach it.

But then I remember: You have plans to give me a future. One day at a time or even one step at a time, I am never in this alone. When I think of the future in this way, some other clichés come to mind: bright, shining promise; filled with potential; great adventure; excitement. Let's go, God—into the future!

No Strings Attached

Watch me with the
very pupil of your eye!
Hide me in the protection
of your wings.

—Psalm 17:8

ACCOMPLISHMENTS are great; it is good to have a goal to reach for. But, Lord, it's greater still to know you love me for who I am. You don't care what abilities I have or what weaknesses I bear. You love me just because you love me—no strings, no conditions. No one else loves like that. I don't earn it, I don't deserve it, and I certainly don't understand it. But I do cherish it, Lord. Thank you for knowing me best and loving me most.

Pressing On

It's not that I have already reached this goal
or have already been perfected, but I pursue
it, so that I may grab hold of it because Christ
grabbed hold of me for just this purpose.

—PHILIPPIANS 3:12

EVERYONE is so proud of me for hanging in there. I'm glad I did. It would sure be easy to sit back and rest, and to coast on all the "congratulations" for a long time. And I think I will relax—for a little while. But help me take the long look, Lord. This may seem like an ending, but it's also a beginning. I want to keep pressing on, just as Jesus did.

Strange Days

Our citizenship is in heaven.
—Philippians 3:20

SOME DAYS are really trying, Lord. Nothing seems to go right: The six o'clock news is especially upsetting; people give me strange looks; I don't even feel "normal." Those days, I have to remind myself that I really am an alien here. My true citizenship is in heaven. This world seems upside down sometimes because it actually isn't my true home.

Don't misunderstand me, God; I'm in no rush to get "home." But on days like today, it surely is comforting to know I'm on my way.

Gratitude

I thank my God every time
I mention you in my prayers.

—Philippians 1:3

I'VE BEEN pretty self-absorbed, looking only toward reaching one goal. Now that I've graduated, I can look back and see so many people who have helped me along the way. Family, friends, teachers, and church members—they all believed in me and invested in me.

I want to be that kind of person, Lord. Shape me into someone who helps others reach their goals. And one other thing, Lord: Teach me to express my gratitude for those people you placed in my life. I want to say "thank you" both to you and to them.

I Need Wisdom

The LORD gives wisdom;
from his mouth
come knowledge
and understanding.

—PROVERBS 2:6

I'M GRATEFUL for my education, Lord. It will help me in so many ways, but I know life's difficulties will require more: I need wisdom. You are the source of wisdom, O God. Help me grow in wisdom and stature, just as Jesus did.

Making a Difference

All of us are looking with unveiled faces at the glory of the Lord as if we were looking in a mirror. We are being transformed into that same image from one degree of glory to the next degree of glory. This comes from the Lord, who is the Spirit.

—2 Corinthians 3:18

IT SEEMS to me that, in some ways, it's easy to make a living but it's hard to make a difference. Lord, whatever I do in the years to come, I want to reflect you. I want people to know I am yours, and I want to lead others to you. Your Spirit can help me make not just a living, but also a difference.

I'm Hurting

Trust in the LORD with all your
heart; don't rely on your own
intelligence.

—PROVERBS 3:5

I'M HURTING, Lord. I know there is more to life than what we see, more than what we know, and more than what we understand. It's that last part I struggle with—situations and circumstances that are beyond my understanding.

I know you have a plan, God; help me trust you even when I can't see it.

Making Decisions

But anyone who needs wisdom should ask God, whose very nature is to give to everyone without a second thought, without keeping score. Wisdom will certainly be given to those who ask.

—JAMES 1:5

I'VE DONE the research. I've made a list of the pros and cons. I've weighed the options. After all of that, I still don't know what to do. And Lord, I don't even know what I want to do.

So here I am, asking for a word from you. You promise wisdom to those who ask, and I'm asking: What is your will? Will you open a door, send a friend, arrange a circumstance? I'm listening; help me hear your voice. I'm confident you will show me the way.

Nursing a Grudge

Make sure that no one misses out
on God's grace. Make sure that no
root of bitterness grows up that might
cause trouble and pollute many people.

—Hebrews 12:15

I'M PRETTY SURE I have just cause to be mad, Lord. They had no right to do what they did to me. But I also know that if I stay mad, it will only hurt me. Bitterness is a deadly cancer. I need to allow people to make mistakes. I need to accept circumstances I can't change. My prayer today is for the grace and acceptance toward others that you have demonstrated toward me.

Going to Church

Don't stop meeting together with other believers, which some people have gotten into the habit of doing. Instead, encourage each other, especially as you see the day drawing near.

—Hebrews 10:25

LORD, I know you designed me to need fellowship. It's not just fun, it's something I have to have to promote my spiritual growth. And yet, it would be so easy to stop going to church, Lord, and to get out of the habit.

Please remind my spirit that I need the fellowship, encouragement, challenge, accountability, and corporate worship that church has to offer. Lead me to the place I can best worship you. And remind me too, Lord, that I have something to offer to the church as well.

Ready for Prayer

Finally, let's draw near to the throne
of favor with confidence so that we can
receive mercy and find grace when
we need help.

—Hebrews 4:16

I HAVEN'T talked with you in a while, Lord. Sometimes I get too busy, too caught up in myself, too stressed out. Other times, I feel too guilty to talk to you. It seems that pressure and guilt push me away from you. And yet I know it's those times when I need to talk to you most.

Remind me, Lord, that you always want to hear from me. I don't have to "get ready" or have all my ducks in a row to talk to you. You always meet me right where I am. I will always find love and mercy when I share my heart with you.

Temptation

But God is faithful. He won't allow you to be tempted beyond your abilities.

—1 Corinthians 10:13b

LORD, you know I have faced temptation in the past, and I'm sure I'll face more in the days to come. I know some of the temptations will be different from those I have faced before. Will I know what to do? What to say?

Help me remember that you are still a source of strength to me, no matter what new challenges I face. With you in my heart, I don't have to do anything I don't want to do. Lead me not into temptation, Lord. And help me see those escape routes.

In the Know

The righteousness that I have
comes from knowing Christ,
the power of his resurrection,
and the participation in his
sufferings. It includes being
conformed to his death.

—PHILIPPIANS 3:10

I SUPPOSE graduating indicates some degree of competency, and that I've acquired some measure of knowledge. I have studied, and I have learned some things. But, Lord, there is so much more to discover about life, about relationships, about you. I want to know you, God. I want to understand your nature and reflect your character and follow as your Spirit leads. I realize the way to know you is to spend time with you. Give me a hunger for your Word and a thirst to spend time talking with you. I'd like to get to know you better.

Finding Purpose

We are God's accomplishment, created in Christ
Jesus to do good things. God planned for these good
things to be the way that we live our lives.

—Ephesians 2:10

DEAR GOD, I sometimes wonder if what I do is important. Does it matter to anyone? Is any accomplishment of lasting value? Remind me, when I have these thoughts, that I am your creation, Lord. You have very important things prepared for me to do, things that may make an eternal difference for someone. Show me what you would have me do, and give me the desire to do it.

New Friends

Love each other like the members
of your family. Be the best at
showing honor to each other.

—ROMANS 12:10

I HAVE some of the best friends in the world. They have been supportive, encouraging, and faithful. It's hard to entertain the thought that I should be open to making new friends when I already have the best! But, Lord, I know I need fellowship to survive. Give me a heart that is open to every person you place in my life, not just to those I've already found it easy to love. Give me the kind of fellowship that will challenge and nurture me just as you do. Help me grow to be a person who values love and honor, and teach me what it means to be such a friend.

Expressing My Anger

Know this, my dear brothers and sisters:
everyone should be quick to listen,
slow to speak, and slow to grow angry.
This is because an angry person doesn't
produce God's righteousness.

—James 1:19-20

I GET so upset! Sometimes it's about circumstances that make no sense; sometimes people are unkind or just get on my last nerve. I find myself near the boiling point, and once in a while, I even explode. Then I feel guilty.

Lord, I know that you designed us to have emotions—joy, pain, and even anger. But I need to know when and if I should express my feelings. I want to be controlled not by my anger, but instead by your Spirit. Give me a spirit of grace and acceptance regarding people and circumstances that are beyond my control. When I speak and when I act, let me do so in a godly way.

Social Action

It is a sin when someone
knows the right thing to do
and doesn't do it.

—James 4:17

DEAR GOD,

They say you can tell a lot about a person by looking at what he or she gets upset about. Someone who gets angry about his or her own concerns does not have the same strength of character as the person who gets angry about injustice toward others. I want to be a person of strong character and compassion. I want to be someone who attempts to right wrongs and to act on conviction. Don't let me have a passive faith, God. Let me demonstrate faith in action.

Foot in Mouth

Don't let any foul words come out of your mouth. Only say what is helpful when it is needed for building up the community so that it benefits those who hear what you say.

—Ephesians 4:29

I STUCK MY FOOT in my mouth, and I said something unkind. How is it that I get my mouth in gear before my mind? I fail to recognize the power my words have—for good and for bad. Funny thing is, I've never failed to notice how powerful are the words others say about me.

God, there's no way to control my tongue without your help. Through the power of your Spirit, make my words powerful and positive. I want to be someone who encourages and builds others up.

Sing a Song of Praise

Speak to each other with psalms,
hymns, and spiritual songs;
sing and make music to
the LORD in your hearts.

—Ephesians 5:19

LORD,

What a wonderful gift is music! Thank you for the means to express my mood, lift my spirits, and praise your name. You have truly put a song in my heart today; I lift my song to praise you for who you are.

Walking in the Spirit

If we live by the Spirit,
let's follow the Spirit.

—Galatians 5:25

I'M A GRADUATE now. Does that mean I'm smarter? More successful? Or just more educated? Some people treat me differently since graduation, as if I gained maturity with the diploma. I don't feel any more mature.

I'm not really sure how I'm supposed to feel, I just know how I do feel: confident one day and apprehensive the next. I know I've accomplished something, but I'm unsure about what happens next. But I'm certain of one thing that hasn't changed, God: I need you in my life. Whatever I'm supposed to feel or do or be, I pray that I will be led by your Spirit.

Trust

Trust in the LORD with
all your heart;
don't rely on your own
intelligence.

—PROVERBS 3:5

I FEEL adventurous today, Lord. I'm anxious to begin an exciting new journey. I have some concerns about moving on, about leaving friends and family and the comfort zone I've been in for so long. But today, God, I want to find out if I am as independent as I feel at this place in my life. Teach me how to nurture this independent spirit and yet still rely completely on you. Teach me to trust.

Trouble

Please let your faithful love
comfort me, according to
what you've said
to your servant.

—Psalm 119:76

I'VE MADE another mess. How many times, God, have I had to ask you to bail me out "just this once more"? Well, here I am again. I'm not asking you to take away the consequences of my actions; I know you don't work that way. But I do need to feel you near me as I go through a very difficult time. Even when I mess up, you never fail me, Lord. Thank you for being a never-ending source of comfort.

No Fear

"I've commanded you to be brave and strong, haven't I? Don't be alarmed or terrified, because the LORD your God is with you wherever you go."

—JOSHUA 1:9

DEAR LORD,
I'm feeling very anxious today. I can't put my finger on the reason, but I'm nervous and afraid. I'm guilty of thinking that the more I know about what's going to happen, the more control I have; you and I both know that's just not true. You are the one in control, and you promise to be with me. I will not be terrified; I will not be discouraged; I will be strong and courageous knowing you are with me.

New Ideas

So live in Christ Jesus the Lord in the same way as you received him. Be rooted and built up in him, be established in faith, and overflow with thanksgiving just as you were taught.

—Colossians 2:6-7

I KNOW I'm going to be facing some new ideas, attitudes, and philosophies, Lord. Some of them could be wonderful, some harmful, some challenging. You have given me a rich heritage of faith. I want to be open-minded and at the same time remain true and faithful in my walk with you. Help me embrace what will strengthen my faith and reject that which won't.

Loneliness

When you search for me,
yes, search for me
with all your heart,
you will find me.

—Jeremiah 29:13

I DON'T LIKE this feeling at all, God. I'm feeling alone, even in a classroom full of people. I know the only cure is to make a connection. So here I am, ready for a heart-to-heart with you. One of the best things I can do is offer you my praise, and I do. You are caring, loving, forgiving, and merciful. And best of all, you are so very near. I thank you and praise you. And I don't feel so alone anymore.

Distractions

Don't love the world or the things in the world. If anyone loves the world, the love of the Father is not in them.

—1 John 2:15

DEAR GOD,

This is a confusing place to be. The world says to get rich; you say to live a rich life. The world says beauty is what counts; you say to look at the heart. The world says to strive to be first; you say the first shall be last. The world says to look out for number one; you say, "Love one another." See what I mean, Lord? It is so easy to get distracted from what really matters in life.

I want you to be first, Lord. Teach me how to be in the world but not of the world.

Hand-Me-Downs

"So, since we have been made righteous by his grace, we can inherit the hope for eternal life."

—Titus 3:7

I APPRECIATE the things that have been handed down to me from my family. I don't mean jewelry or furniture; people say I have my mother's smile and my father's sense of fairness. I'm grateful for those things.

One thing my family couldn't hand down to me is my relationship with you, Lord. Regardless of whether my family has been connected to the church, I am the only one who can decide whether to be connected to you. So I thank you, Lord, for my family and the faith heritage they have given me, and for giving me the freedom to accept you on my own.

Undercover Christian

I'm not ashamed of the gospel:
it is God's own power for salvation
to all who have faith in God.

—Romans 1:16a

TODAY I had the chance to take a stand for you, Lord, but I knew there would be no applause. I knew I'd have to explain why I believe what I do, and I just couldn't bear the thought that I might be laughed at. I don't want to turn people off, to be coercive or oppressive or heavy-handed. But I do want to find a way to share my faith that will take away my fear and will serve you best.

I am tired of being an undercover Christian, God. I pray that you will give me both the boldness and the sensitivity of your Spirit, and that you will teach me what it means to truly witness to others of your power and goodness.

A Real Job

Whatever you do, do it
from the heart for the Lord
and not for people.

—Colossians 3:23

OKAY, I graduated. Now it's time to get a job. I'm not sure what it will be. I'm not sure where to look. Lord, I'm not even sure what I want to do! But I know that whatever I do, whatever my job, enthusiasm will be essential.

Lead me to that new job, Lord. I promise that I will work from my heart.

Best Book

"Never stop speaking about this Instruction scroll. Recite it day and night so you can carefully obey everything written in it. Then you will accomplish your objectives and you will succeed."

—Joshua 1:8

I'VE READ a lot of books. I've done a lot of studying, and I hope to do more. I pray, dear God, that you will give me a hunger for "The Book"—the Bible. I want to learn more about you, your character, your nature. I want to study your word—and I want to live it.

First Impressions

"God doesn't look at things like humans do. Humans see only what is visible to the eyes, but the LORD sees into the heart."

—1 SAMUEL 16:7B, C

I AM going to be meeting many new people, Lord. I make quick judgments about others. I take in the first few words they say, or what they do, or what they look like, or what they are wearing, and I put a label on them in my mind. How unfair that is! You don't look at people that way, God. You look on the heart. Help me see others as you do.

Armor of God

Finally, be strengthened by the Lord and his powerful strength. Put on God's armor so that you can make a stand against the tricks of the devil.

—Ephesians 6:10-11

GOD, I'm fighting a lot of battles—stress, pressure, temptations, problems. I need your strength. Help me put on your armor. Help me remember that the enemy is not other people, but the force of evil. In my weakness, use your power to make me strong.

Earning Extra Credit

Let's not get tired of doing good,
because in time we'll have a
harvest if we don't give up.

—Galatians 6:9

SERVING GOD and serving others—that's what I want my life to be about. But I have this hang-up about getting credit for it, God. I want to be sure everyone knows about the good things I do, and that defeats the whole purpose. I pray that you will mold me into the kind of person who helps others because they need it, not for praise or applause. Teach me to love giving and serving—anonymously.

Inconvenience

Carry each other's burdens and so you will
fulfill the law of Christ.

—Galatians 6:2

IT'S EASY to be helpful when it's convenient or when it doesn't cost anything or when it doesn't take much time. But somehow, Lord, I don't think that is what you had in mind for us. It's certainly not the example you set for us. I'm not sure how to determine the amount of time or energy or resources to invest in someone who needs my help, but I know that you will guide me, Lord, in my quest to find out.

Changing the World

A little yeast works through
the whole lump of dough.

—Galatians 5:9

I'D LOVE to change the world. I'd love to be a person of such charisma, such influence, such purpose that I could turn the world upside down for you, God. Just thinking about it overwhelms me. And then I realize that you don't call me to do any of that. You have called me to be a world-changer, Lord—but by one word, one action, one person at a time.

Meeting the Requirements

He has told you, human one, what is
good and what the LORD requires from you:
to do justice, embrace faithful love,
and walk humbly with your God.

—MICAH 6:8

YOU don't get to graduate unless you meet certain requirements. What about your requirements, God? Will you teach me what they are and how to meet them? I know you would never ask me to do something that I am not capable of doing. I'm willing, Lord. It's past time for "class" to start.

Blank Slate

But if we confess our sins, he is faithful and just to forgive us our sins and cleanse us from everything we've done wrong.

—1 JOHN 1:9

MERCIFUL GOD,
I thank you for the way you forgive. I don't understand it. But because Jesus paid the price, you always forgive me and clear my account. No one else does that. Blank slate. Empty set. Null and void. Erased disk.

Thank you, thank you, thank you!

Gentleness

Let your gentleness show
in your treatment of all people.
The Lord is near.

—Philippians 4:5

THIS IS an aggressive, go-get-'em world. Gentleness is not a quality greatly admired by society as a whole. But it seems to me that individuals value gentleness very much. I love gentle people. Jesus was gentle; gentleness is one of the fruits of the Spirit.

Loving God, you urge us to be not aggressors, but rather people with gentle spirits. I think gentleness reflects great strength. And I pray that I can be a person with a gentle spirit.

High Anxiety

Don't be anxious about anything; rather
bring up all of your requests to God in
your prayers and petitions, along with
giving thanks.

—Philippians 4:6

I HAVE been obsessing about this problem, Lord. I've turned it over and over in my mind. It has kept me awake at night; it has given me headaches and stomachaches. And all my worrying hasn't helped me find a solution. I'm wasting my energy dwelling on something that's out of my control. So now, dear God, I ask you to take this anxiety from me. And I will refuse to think about my problem anymore unless I'm thankfully praying about it to you.
Amen and amen.

Praiseworthy Things

From now on, brothers and sisters, if anything is excellent and if anything is admirable, focus your thoughts on these things: all that is true, all that is holy, all that is just, all that is pure, all that is lovely, and all that is worthy of praise.

—PHILIPPIANS 4:8

THERE ARE a lot of voices out there, Lord. Television, movies, and music can all present some pretty negative images for my mind to dwell on. Then there's the news, the papers, and magazines. I don't think it's unhealthy for me to be exposed to things; to avoid them completely, I'd practically have to live in a cave! But I do know that I need some discernment, Lord, some judgment and perspective. And I need you to help me focus on those things that are "worthy of praise."

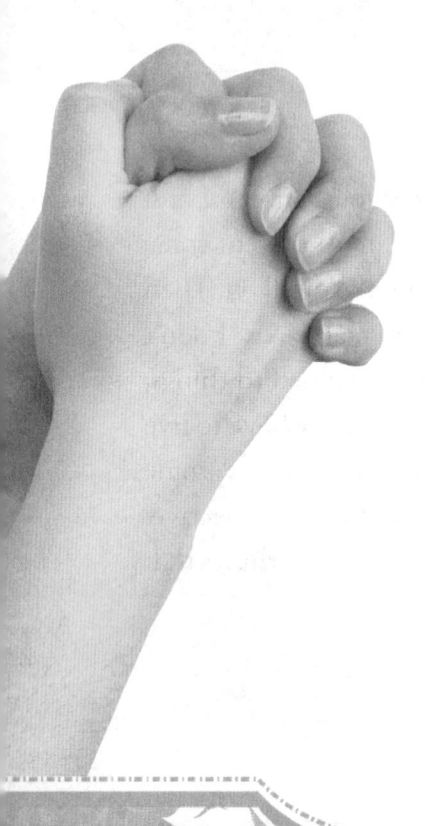

Silent Prayer

Why do you stand so far away,
LORD, hiding yourself in
troubling times?

—PSALM 10:1

I'M HAVING trouble praying today, Lord. I've got major problems, and you seem very far away. My heart is so heavy, I just don't know what to say. I know you haven't gone anywhere; I'm the one who moved. Please know my heart and give me words. Comfort me with your peace.

Doubts

Faith is the reality of
what we hope for,
the proof of what we don't see.

—Hebrews 11:1

IS IT silly for me to pray when I'm having some doubts, Lord? I need you to help me through these new questions. I've been questioning things I always just accepted before.

Dear God, I'm asking you to use this probing to make my faith stronger. Help me be sure and certain. I want a faith that is strong enough to hold up to the light.

Living Praise

Praise God in his mighty acts!
Praise God as suits
his incredible greatness!

—Psalm 150:2

MIGHTY GOD, I love you so much. I praise you for what you do and for who you are. You love and forgive. You are holy and righteous. You are worthy of my thanks and praise. I praise you with my words, and I praise you with my heart. Help me praise you with all of my life.

A New Day

This is the day the LORD acted;
we will rejoice and celebrate in it!

—Psalm 118:24

YOU ARE A GOD of second chances—and third and thirtieth and so on. And I am someone who needs all of those chances. Chances to make a fresh start. Chances to move on. Chances to leave some baggage behind. I get a "do-over" anytime I need one. Jesus made that possible for me.

This is a new day. And thanks to you, Lord, it's a new chance.

Surprise Ending

I'm sure about this: the one who started a good work in you will stay with you to complete the job by the day of Christ Jesus.

—Philippians 1:6

DEAR GOD, I'm so glad that you have a lot more in store for me. Milestones are great, but I'd hate to think my graduation was the end of this road. Lord, I know you didn't bring me to this place to leave me to my own devices. There are things in your plan for tomorrow that I could never even imagine today. Give me an expectant heart to discover what you will continue to do with all you have invested in me.

Amazing Grace

Be kind, compassionate, and forgiving to each other, in the same way God forgave you in Christ.

—Ephesians 4:32

I WAS BOTH angered and hurt by someone today, Lord. It's funny how, when I say something unkind or provocative, people are just supposed to understand. I always have a "good" reason; it's never "intentional." However, when others are hurtful to me, I fail to show them the kind of grace I expect them to show me.

Your grace is always there, O God—for all of us. Teach me to be tolerant and patient and gracious, Lord. Teach me to be like you.

The Gift of Laughter

A joyful heart helps healing.

—Proverbs 17:22a

TODAY my friends and I got amused, and before I knew it, I was laughing out of control. I laughed until tears were streaming down my face! I hadn't laughed really hard in a long time, and it felt so good. What wonderful gifts you have given me in laughter and friendship. Thank you, Lord, for lifting my spirit.

Accountability

As iron sharpens iron, so friends sharpen each other's faces.

—Proverbs 27:17

TODAY a friend hurt my feelings with her honesty, Lord. But after the sting began to fade, I examined her comments and discovered some truth. And as I bring this before you, I realize the need I have for someone who will tell me the truth and hold me accountable. Thank you, God, for the maturity to recognize this. And even more, thank you for the very wise friend in my life.

Priorities

"Instead, desire first and foremost God's kingdom and God's righteousness, and all these things will be given to you as well."

—Matthew 6:33

I SAY that I want you first in my life, Lord. But today I looked at my calendar and my checkbook. I had to look long and hard to find any evidence that you are a top priority. Please understand: I don't want the kind of faith that's compartmentalized, where certain things are dedicated to you and others are not. I really want to invite you to be a part of everything I do—and everything I am.

A Childlike Faith

"I assure you that if you don't turn your lives around and become like this little child, you will definitely not enter the kingdom of heaven."

—Matthew 18:3

CHILDREN have one quality that I really admire: vulnerability. Children haven't learned yet to put on a mask or cover up hurt or deny weakness. They are who they are, and they're not afraid to be true to that. I think that sometimes I make faith so complicated. I need a childlike faith that says, "I'm yours, Lord, all the way!"

Who can I be vulnerable with, if not with you? Here I am, God, I'm all yours—warts and all!

Obedience

"If you love me, you will keep my commandments."
—John 14:15

I'VE BEEN confused about this obedience thing for so long. For years, Lord, I thought I should obey so that I could go to heaven. But if that were true, why would Jesus have had to suffer on the cross? Now, things seem clearer to me: I obey you in response to your gift of salvation, not to achieve it. A life of obedience is a grateful heart expressing itself to you. And obedience means love.

Also available from Abingdon Press

Scripture & Prayers

A Moment with God

FOR SUNDAY
SCHOOL TEACHERS

Scripture & Prayers

A Moment with God
FOR TEACHERS

Scripture & Prayers

A Moment with God
FOR TEENS

Scripture & Prayers

A Moment with God
FOR THOSE WHO GRIEVE

A Moment with God
FOR MOTHERS

Scripture & Prayers